Maps AND Mapping

MAPPING
PHYSICAL GEOGRAPHY

BY
ALEX BRINDED

KidHaven PUBLISHING

Published in 2020 by KidHaven Publishing, an Imprint of Greenhaven Publishing, LLC
353 3rd Avenue, Suite 255, New York, NY 10010

Written by: Alex Brinded
Edited by: Holly Duhig
Designed by: Drue Rintoul

Cataloging-in-Publication Data

Names: Brinded, Alex.
Title: Mapping physical geography / Alex Brinded.
Description: New York : KidHaven Publishing, 2020. | Series: Maps and mapping | Includes glossary and index.
Identifiers: ISBN 9781534531109 (pbk.) | ISBN 9781534530218 (library bound) | ISBN 9781534531512 (6 pack) | ISBN 9781534531048 (ebook)
Subjects: LCSH: Physical geography--Juvenile literature. | Cartography--Juvenile literature.
Classification: LCC GB58.B756 2020 | DDC 551.43'2--dc23

Image Credits
All images are courtesy of Shutterstock.com, unless otherwise specified. With thanks to Getty Images, Thinkstock Photo and iStockphoto.
Front Cover – Andrew Mayovskyy, Budkov Denis. 2 – Park Jae Beom. 4&5 – Rainer Lesniewski, Artisticco, Abscent. 6&7 – Intrepix, Rainer Lesniewski, zeffirka84, Schwabenblitz. 8&9 – gallimaufry, RTimages, AKaiser. 10&11 – By Strebe (Own work) [CC BY-SA 3.0 (https://creativecommons.org/licenses/by-sa/3.0)], via Wikimedia Commons, CC BY-SA 3.0, https://commons.wikimedia.org/w/index.php?curid=117566, Volodymyr Nikulishyn. 12&13 – Thomas Römer/OpenStreetMap data [ODbL (http://opendatacommons.org/licenses/odbl/1.0/) or CC BY-SA 3.0 (https://creativecommons.org/licenses/by-sa/3.0)], via Wikimedia Commons, By Eric Gaba (Sting), translated by Bamse (CC BY-SA 2.5 (https://creativecommons.org/licenses/by-sa/2.5)], via Wikimedia Commons, Peter Hermes Furian. 14&15 – Peter Hermes Furian, Steven Wright, By Djexplo (Own work) [CC0], via Wikimedia Commons, AVS-Images, By No machine-readable author provided. Obersachse assumed (based on copyright claims). [GFDL (http://www.gnu.org/copyleft/fdl.html) or CC-BY-SA-3.0 (http://creativecommons.org/licenses/by-sa/3.0/)], via Wikimedia Commons. 16&17 – Mopic, VPales, slhy, brichuas. 18&19 – Designua, ArCaLu, Volodymyr Burdiak, gillmar, StevanZZ. 20&21 – AlexLMX, Vadim Sadovski, Vladimir Prusakov. 22&23 – By Osvaldocangaspadilla (Own work) [Public domain], via Wikimedia Commons, Designua, Peter Hermes Furian, By Gringer (talk) 23:52, 10 February 2009 (UTC) (vector data from [1]) [Public domain], via Wikimedia Commons. 24&25 – OBJM, Designua, By NGranderson (Own work) [CC BY-SA 3.0 (https://creativecommons.org/licenses/by-sa/3.0)], via Wikimedia Commons, Cico. 26&27 – Saulius Damulevicius, Galyna Andrushko, Fotos593, Paul K (via Flickr.com). 28&29 – Naschy, Voran, Benjamin Marin Rubio, creativemarc.

Printed in the United States of America

CPSIA compliance information: Batch #BS19KL: For further information contact Greenhaven Publishing LLC, New York, New York at 1-844-317-7404.

CONTENTS

Words that look like **this** are explained in the glossary on page 31.

What Is a Map?

Maps are diagrams that show parts of the world and how they are connected. Maps can show a big area, like the entire world, or a small area, like a town or village. Some maps only show natural **features** of the landscape like mountains and rivers. Other maps show where buildings and roads are. Some maps only show specific areas. For example, amusement park maps help visitors find their way around the park and plan their day.

With this map, a visitor can see where all the rides and roller coasters are and how to get to each one.

CHOOSING WHAT TO MAP

Maps are a way of displaying information. Some maps, such as road maps, display information that helps people find their way from one place to another, but not all maps are made for traveling. Maps are also used to show information about **landmarks**, natural features, animals, or people. A person who makes maps, called a cartographer, decides what to put on a map depending on the information the map is trying to show.

This map of Africa shows some natural features, such as vegetation, but not towns or cities.

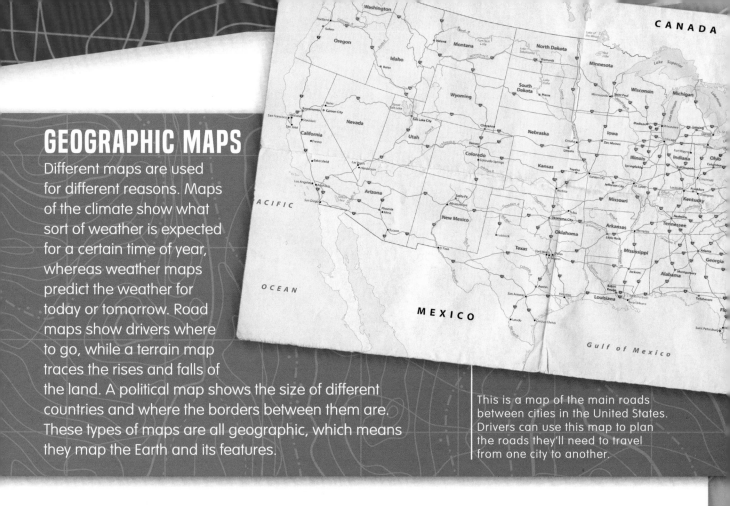

GEOGRAPHIC MAPS

Different maps are used for different reasons. Maps of the climate show what sort of weather is expected for a certain time of year, whereas weather maps predict the weather for today or tomorrow. Road maps show drivers where to go, while a terrain map traces the rises and falls of the land. A political map shows the size of different countries and where the borders between them are. These types of maps are all geographic, which means they map the Earth and its features.

This is a map of the main roads between cities in the United States. Drivers can use this map to plan the roads they'll need to travel from one city to another.

Non-Geographic Maps

Maps can also be used to map non-geographical things. There are tree maps that show the order of events and how they are related. For example, a family tree map shows when people who are related were born. Mind maps are ways to come up with ideas that are linked to one main topic. The police use maps that link different pieces of **evidence** together to work out how a crime was committed.

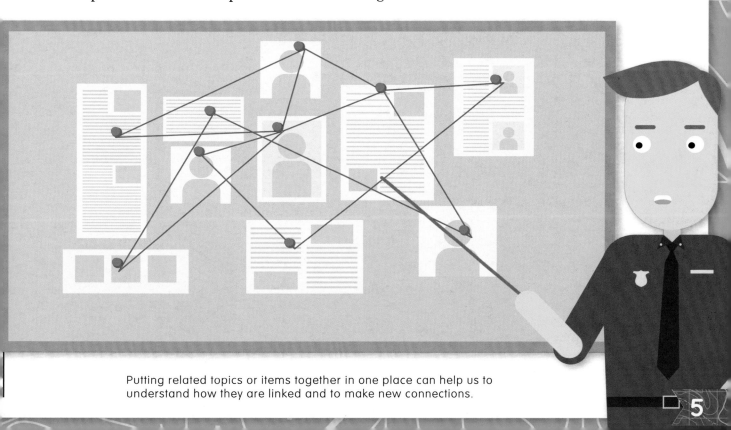

Putting related topics or items together in one place can help us to understand how they are linked and to make new connections.

MAPPING
LANDSCAPES

WHAT FEATURES?

Cartographers draw maps from a "bird's-eye view," as if looking down from above. They have to be careful to make sure that all the relevant features are included. The features that are relevant depend on the type of map being made. If the map is meant to show the natural features of an area, mountains and coastlines need highlighting. If the map is meant to show what towns and cities look like, buildings and roads need to be shown clearly.

This map of France shows different types of terrain.

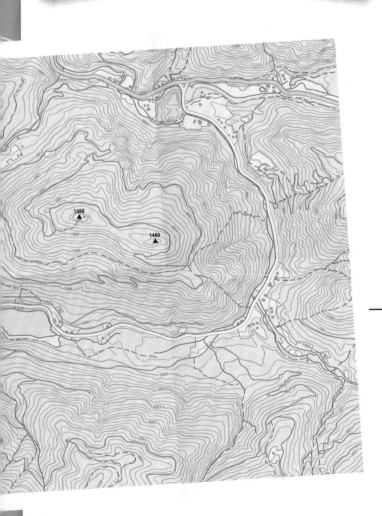

Topographic Maps

Topographic maps show the terrain of an area, which means the features of its landscape, such as forests or grass plains. They also show the height differences between different areas. The height of an area, known as its elevation, is measured from **sea level**. The slopes around an area of elevation are shown either by using contour lines or shading in the area.

The peak of each mountain is marked by a small triangle with the height written alongside.

A CONTOUR LINE CONNECTS THE POINTS IN AN AREA THAT ARE OF THE SAME HEIGHT.

Traveling over Terrain

A topographic map is useful when traveling. Knowing where all the hills or rivers are helps when planning a journey. A terrain map will show travelers when the way ahead is **impassable**. For example, a mountain range could block your route. The terrain also affects weather conditions – mountains have **changeable** weather and it can rain and snow unexpectedly. By checking a topographic map, travelers can wear and pack the right clothes they'll need for their trip.

WORKING WITH TOPOGRAPHIC MAPS

Topographic maps are used for lots of different jobs. **Conservationists** protect parts of the environment by separating areas of land. Farmers must plan where to plant crops or keep **livestock**, because the terrain of an area affects the amount of sunlight and water a field gets. **Architects** and town planners design buildings to be suitable for the terrain. Even pilots need to be aware of the changes in landscape when they are flying low.

This map of New Zealand shows the mountains in brown. Which island has more mountains, North or South Island?

The pilots of this plane need to make sure they fly above these mountains.

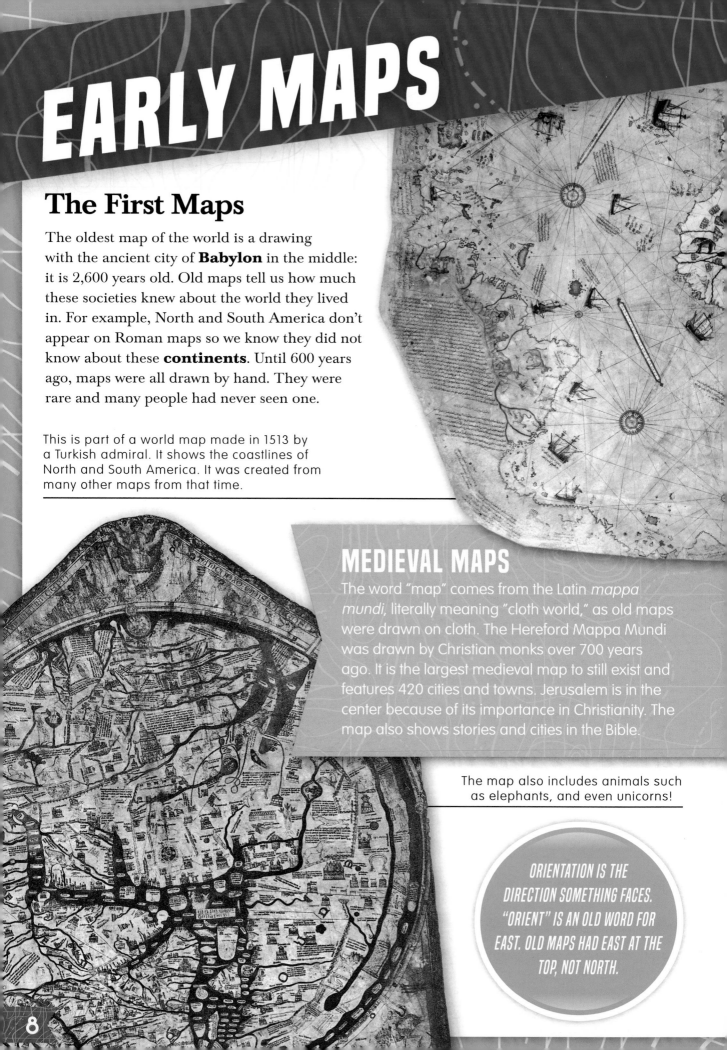

EARLY MAPS

The First Maps

The oldest map of the world is a drawing with the ancient city of **Babylon** in the middle: it is 2,600 years old. Old maps tell us how much these societies knew about the world they lived in. For example, North and South America don't appear on Roman maps so we know they did not know about these **continents**. Until 600 years ago, maps were all drawn by hand. They were rare and many people had never seen one.

This is part of a world map made in 1513 by a Turkish admiral. It shows the coastlines of North and South America. It was created from many other maps from that time.

MEDIEVAL MAPS

The word "map" comes from the Latin *mappa mundi*, literally meaning "cloth world," as old maps were drawn on cloth. The Hereford Mappa Mundi was drawn by Christian monks over 700 years ago. It is the largest medieval map to still exist and features 420 cities and towns. Jerusalem is in the center because of its importance in Christianity. The map also shows stories and cities in the Bible.

The map also includes animals such as elephants, and even unicorns!

ORIENTATION IS THE DIRECTION SOMETHING FACES. "ORIENT" IS AN OLD WORD FOR EAST. OLD MAPS HAD EAST AT THE TOP, NOT NORTH.

THE FIRST ATLAS

Gerard Mercator was a Belgian mapmaker. In 1569, he made the first map of the world with all the continents included. Before Mercator's Atlas, the entire Earth was usually shown on round globes. As it's impossible to accurately draw a round, **three-dimensional (3-D)** object on a flat surface, a world map is never 100% correct. The cartographer has to stretch and squash different parts of a map in order to project it onto a flat surface.

Size Differences

In the past, sailors relied on maps for **navigation** and directions. The Mercator **projection** was made for sailors to find directions across large distances. By using the map and their compass, they could find the direction they needed to follow all the way to their destination. To make this possible, Mercator changed the size and shape of the continents on the globe. Nowadays, world maps are not used for sailing, and are instead used to show all countries as accurately as possible.

Being able to draw the map flat meant that it could be published in books and lots more people could see it.

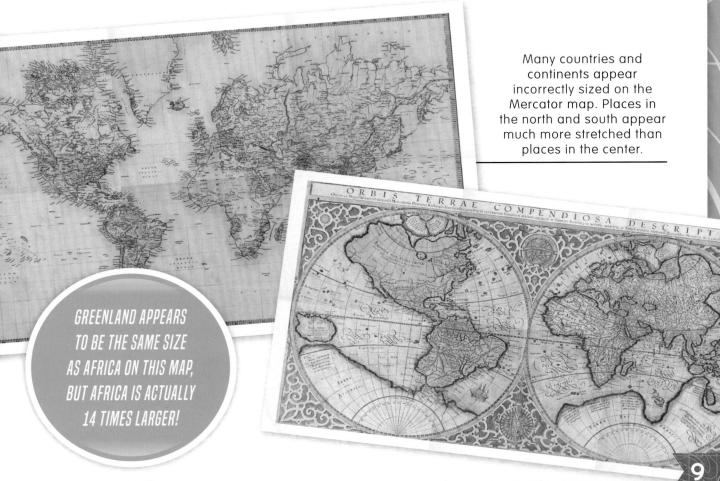

Many countries and continents appear incorrectly sized on the Mercator map. Places in the north and south appear much more stretched than places in the center.

GREENLAND APPEARS TO BE THE SAME SIZE AS AFRICA ON THIS MAP, BUT AFRICA IS ACTUALLY 14 TIMES LARGER!

The Gall-Peters Projection

The Gall-Peters projection is named after two men, James Gall and Arno Peters. In 1885, James Gall wanted to create a map with the correct sizes of all the continents. Nearly 100 years later, Arno Peters drew the same map without realizing it already existed. The Gall-Peters projection shows the real size of the continents but changes their shape. Europe and the U.S. are much more accurate, but any land in the middle of the world is stretched and squashed.

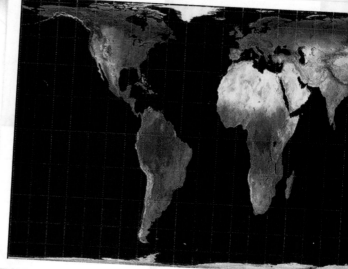

Look how much bigger Africa and South America are on this map than on the Mercator projection.

THE WINKEL TRIPEL PROJECTION

In 1921, Oswald Winkel made the Winkel Tripel map to show the shape and size of countries more accurately. The Winkel Tripel projection is very close to showing the true size and shape of the continents, but because it changes the angles, it is not useful for navigation. It was only toward the end of the 20th century that this map began to be used, as organizations realized its accuracy was useful for understanding the world.

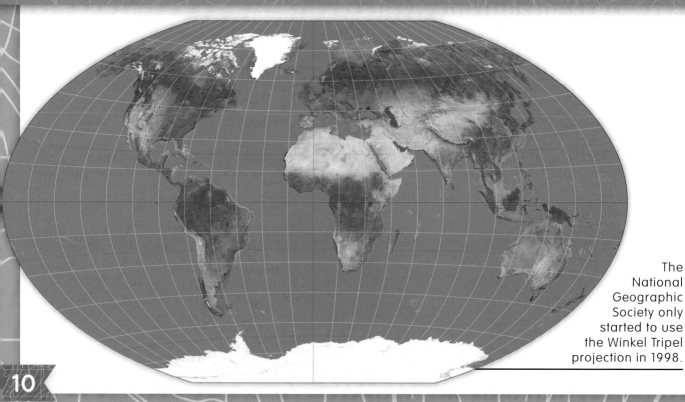

The National Geographic Society only started to use the Winkel Tripel projection in 1998.

A DIFFERENT PERSPECTIVE

A lot of maps show the world with Europe at the center but, as the Earth is round, there is no true center of the globe. We could choose the center of the map to be anywhere. Moving the center of the map makes us see the world in a different way. For example, this map, which shows the Pacific Ocean in the middle, makes us realize just how big it really is.

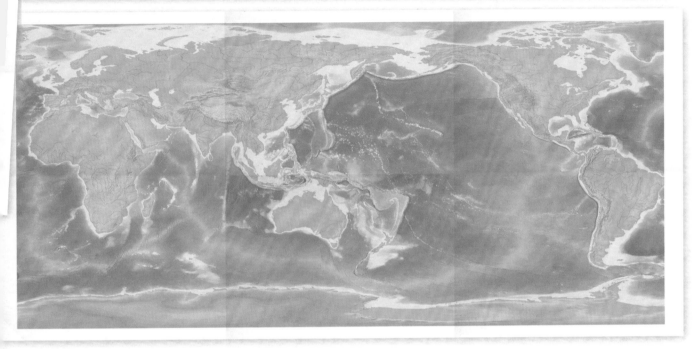

No Way Is Up

The Fuller projection was invented by Buckminster Fuller in 1943. The round Earth is turned into a many-sided shape that is then unfolded. Because the sides are not joined together into a rectangle, the continents don't change shape as much as a Mercator or Gall-Peters projection. It makes it confusing to look at but it does mean no continent is shown in the center. As the oceans are split up, it is a difficult map to use for navigation.

FOLDING THIS MAP TOGETHER WOULD MAKE A 3-D SHAPE.

The smaller white landmass is the Arctic and the bigger one is the Antarctic.

SIZE AND SCALE

What Is Scale?

Scale is the **ratio** between the true size of an area and how it is shown on a map. For example, 1 inch (2.5 cm) on a map can be used to represent 1 mile (1.6 km) in real life. The area that is being drawn has to be shrunk to fit on the map. Using a scale means the area can be shrunk, but the reader can still work out the real distance between any two points on the map.

This large scale map of Vatican City in Rome shows the city state in detail – but using a scale means it fits in this book!

This map of Easter Island in the Pacific Ocean has a scale of 1:372,000. One cm (0.4 inch) on the map equals 372,000 cm (146,457 inches), or 3.72 km (2.3 miles), in real life.

USING SCALE

Using a scale to draw anything that is real and measurable makes the drawing more accurate. Architects and engineers use scale drawings to show exactly what their planned buildings and construction will look like. Using scale means that a drawing is accurate and all the features can be seen. A map is not the same size as the real area, but all the features, such as mountains or valleys, will be in the right place when the map is scaled up.

EASTER ISLAND HAS 887 STONE SCULPTURES OF GIANT HEADS THAT WERE MADE A LONG TIME AGO. THIS MAP SHOWS WHERE THEY ARE LOCATED.

LARGE-SCALE AND SMALL-SCALE MAPS

A large-scale map shows a lot of detail. A small-scale map has a smaller amount of detail and shows a wider area. The cartographer has to choose the scale depending on the size of the area they want to include. A common scale used by large scale maps is 1:25,000. On these maps, every 1 cm (0.4 inch) on represents 25,000 cm (9,842 inches) in real life. A common scale used by small-scale maps is 1:50,000, where 1 cm (0.4 inch) represents 50,000 cm (19,685 inches).

This map of Brazil is a small-scale map because it shows a small amount of detail, but an area so big it includes most of South America.

Using Symbols

Because everything is scaled down on a map, not all landmarks and features of a place can easily fit. The cartographer has to decide what features to focus on. The features are often simplified to be a few symbols or a few letters, to create space on the map. For example, many maps use "Sch" for a school and "Mus" for a museum. Some features are not drawn to scale, as they would be too small and need to be noticeable, such as a river.

HOUSE

DIRECTIONS

CAFÉ

GAS

TELEPHONE

FOOD

LATITUDE AND
LONGITUDE

Get on the Grid

When going somewhere new, it can be hard to find your way. A map can help, but if the place has no name or address, like a hill or field, it's difficult to even find it on the map. This is why maps have grids. Each point on the map then has a grid reference, the specific number of both the horizontal (side to side) and vertical (up and down) lines that cross at the location. Tracing the two lines to where they cross finds the location.

In this map of France, there are large areas apparently with nothing in them. If you were meeting someone there using this map, you wouldn't know where they were.

GETTING YOUR COORDINATES

A grid over a world map is like a grid over a town map, but can be used to find the location of anywhere on Earth. If you tell someone the numbers of the nearest horizontal and vertical lines to where you are, known as your coordinates, they can easily find you. Moving a few feet in any direction changes your coordinates. With this grid we can find where anyone is in the world, even if there isn't a landmark nearby. The horizontal lines are lines of latitude and the vertical lines are lines of longitude.

Both latitude and longitude are measured in degrees or °.

LATITUDE

Zero degrees latitude, or 0°, goes around the middle of the Earth and is called the equator. The equator splits the world into two equal halves; the Northern **Hemisphere** and the Southern Hemisphere. There are 90 degrees to the north of the equator and 90 degrees to the south, all 69 miles (111 km) apart. The degrees of latitude are like loops around the world that get smaller nearer the poles, until 90°N and 90°S are just dots that mark the North and South Poles.

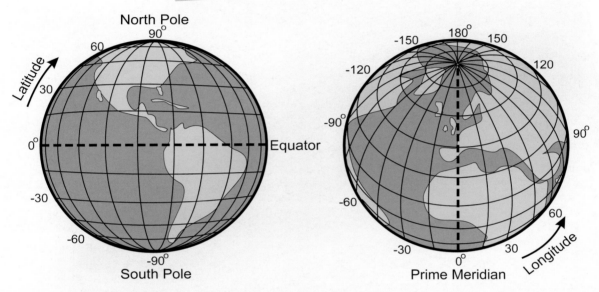

The equator is 0° latitude while the prime meridian is 0° longitude.

Longitude

Zero degrees longitude is the prime meridian and passes through Greenwich, London. This longitude line was chosen as 0° because it was already in use as a reference for navigation. There are 360 longitude lines altogether. There are 179 degrees of longitude to the east of the prime meridian, and 179 to the west. One degree to the west is minus one, or -1°, and one degree to the east is 1°. This means that 180° is on the exact opposite side of the world, so it is called the antimeridian.

The horizontal lines are lines of latitude and the vertical lines are lines of longitude.

MAPPING TIME

Spinning Around the Sun

Day and night happen at different times around the world. It can be daytime in New Zealand while it's nighttime in Spain. Day begins when the sun appears on the horizon. It looks like the sun moves across the sky, but it actually stays fixed while the Earth **orbits** around it. This is similar to being in a car and seeing things outside go backwards, when really the car is moving forwards.

The Earth spins from west to east, so the sun appears on the Eastern horizon as that part of the world spins out of the shadow to face it.

SOLAR TIME

Time used to be measured using sundials. The sun casts a shadow onto a sundial's clockface and, like the hand of a clock, the shadow points to the time that it is. As the sun appears to move across the sky, the shadow moves around the clockface. If the sun appears over the horizon at 7:30 a.m. in St. Petersburg in Russia, it will appear on the horizon later in London because the UK is a long way west of Russia. Sundials tell a different time in places with different longitudes.

The shadow of this sundial points towards the number 15, showing that it is 15:00 hours or 3pm.

KEEPING TIME BY THE SUN

The sun rises two seconds later for every kilometer further west that you travel. For example, Bristol is over two degrees west of London, over 138 miles (222 km), and the sun rises 10 minutes later there than in London. Each place used to measure its own solar time. A local clock, such as a church clock, would keep the time so local people could set their watches by it.

The sun rises in the east and sets in the west.

When train travel was invented, they passed though many different places very quickly. Because each place had different solar times, passengers would have to reset their watches at each stop. About 150 years ago, it was decided that all UK clocks would be set to Greenwich Mean Time (GMT). GMT is the solar time as seen from Greenwich Royal Observatory in London, which sits on 0° longitude. This means that when the sun rises at 7 a.m. in Greenwich it is now also 7 a.m. in Bristol, even though the sun rises 10 minutes later in Bristol.

GMT IS IN THE MIDDLE BAND, WITH 0 AT THE TOP. EVERY BAND TO THE LEFT IS AN EXTRA HOUR BEHIND, AND EVERY BAND TO THE RIGHT IS AN HOUR AHEAD.

This is a map of the agreed world time zones.
All the places within each band observe the same time.

HABITATS AND BIOMES

Ecosystems and Biomes

Ecosystems are parts of the environment where the living things rely on each other for survival. They can be small, like a pond, or large, like a forest. Ecosystems are home to different plants and animals that have adapted to the conditions.

The ten largest ecosystems, called biomes, exist over large areas of land, including across continents. Biomes have different climates, depending on how far they are from the equator, how far they are from the sea, and how far above sea level they are.

Arctic Ocean

Arctic Ocean

Atlantic Ocean

Pacific Ocean

Pacific Ocean

Indian Ocean

Southern Ocean

Southern Ocean

KEY
- Ice sheet and polar desert
- Tundra
- Taiga
- Montane
- Mixed and deciduous forest
- Tropical rain forest
- Steppe
- Savanna
- Desert
- Mediterranean vegetation

The different colors show the different biomes. You can see where each biome exists across the continents. For example, the tundra can be seen as a light purple stripe across the north of the world.

FOREST BIOMES

- Tropical rain forests are hot and humid, and are home to half of all animal and plant species. They are near the equator in Central America, South America, Africa, and Asia.

- Deciduous forests are mild and wet, with trees that lose their leaves in winter. They exist across Europe and the U.S.

- Coniferous forest, or the taiga, is the largest biome. It can be found in Scandinavia, Russia, and Canada. It has a cool summer and a long winter during which the trees keep their leaves.

Brown bears live in coniferous forest.

18

DESERTS, STEPPES, AND SAVANNAS

- Deserts are hot and dry, but cold at night. They are found near the equator where there is the most sunshine. The Sahara in North Africa is almost as big as the U.S.

- A steppe is a dry or grassy plain with no trees. The Eurasian steppe is huge and goes from Hungary to China.

- The savannah is hot, tropical grassland with some scrubs and trees. It can be found in Central Africa, Northern Australia, and South America.

The savanna is the natural habitat for giraffes.

Polar bears are one of the biggest species of mammals that live in the tundra.

Tundra, Polar Desert, Montane, and Mediterranean

- Tundra is very cold land, with very few plants or animals, near the North and South Poles.

- Polar deserts are dry and freezing cold, with no vegetation. They are found in Antarctica and the Arctic.

- Montane is a biome created by mountains. The cold temperature at high altitude limits the growing season of plants and trees.

- The Mediterranean biome is named after the warm and pleasant climate around the Mediterranean, where lots of animals and plants live, but also occurs in South Africa and southern Australia.

The Mediterranean biome is warm, pleasant, and very green.

WHAT IN THE WORLD
IS IT MADE OF?

THE EARTH IS NOT COMPLETELY SOLID. IT IS MADE OF FOUR MAIN LAYERS.

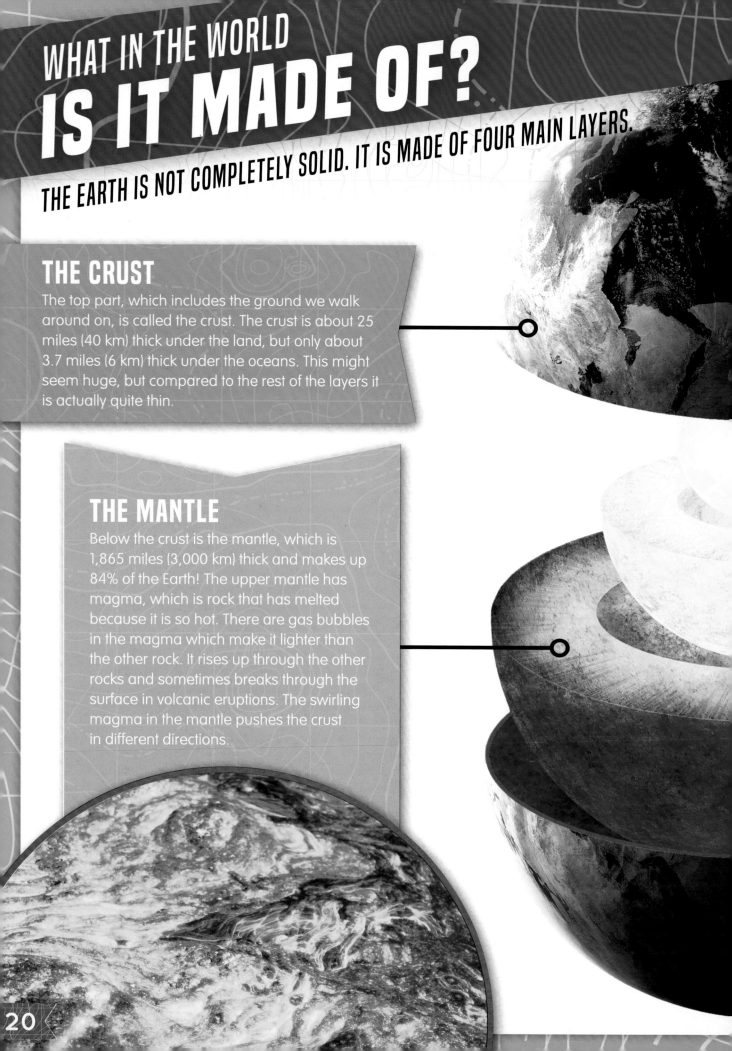

THE CRUST

The top part, which includes the ground we walk around on, is called the crust. The crust is about 25 miles (40 km) thick under the land, but only about 3.7 miles (6 km) thick under the oceans. This might seem huge, but compared to the rest of the layers it is actually quite thin.

THE MANTLE

Below the crust is the mantle, which is 1,865 miles (3,000 km) thick and makes up 84% of the Earth! The upper mantle has magma, which is rock that has melted because it is so hot. There are gas bubbles in the magma which make it lighter than the other rock. It rises up through the other rocks and sometimes breaks through the surface in volcanic eruptions. The swirling magma in the mantle pushes the crust in different directions.

THE CORE

Below the mantle is the outer core, which is liquid metal. It's about 1,430 miles (2,300 km) thick and incredibly hot, at 7,952°F (4,400°C). The inner core is the center of the Earth. It is a 1,550-mile-wide (2,500 km) ball of iron and nickel. At 11,012°F (6,100°C), it is hot enough to be a liquid, but the weight of the world **compresses** it into a solid.

The metal core is so hot it would be a liquid if it wasn't compressed down into a solid.

Cross-Sections and Samples

One way to map 3-D objects is to take a cross-section. A cross-section is a diagram of an object where it is shown split in half so that we can see inside it. Cross-section diagrams of the Earth show us how much of the Earth is made up of crust and how much is the mantle and core. We know what is inside the Earth thanks to sensors and samples, which can involve drilling down into the earth or **glaciers**.

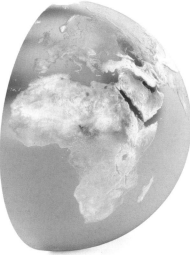

A CHANGING WORLD

Matching Coastlines

Alfred Wegener was a German scientist. In the early 1900s, he noticed that the coastlines of South America and Africa looked similar – like two puzzle pieces! He thought all seven continents were once joined like a giant puzzle but had drifted apart. Other clues include:

1. Fossils of the same species being found on different continents.

2. Antarctic coal – With coal being made of dead trees, and it being too cold near the South Pole for trees, the climate must have been warmer.

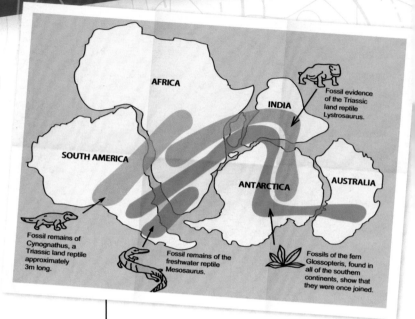

AFRICA

INDIA

Fossil evidence of the Triassic land reptile Lystrosaurus.

SOUTH AMERICA

ANTARCTICA

AUSTRALIA

Fossil remains of Cynognathus, a Triassic land reptile approximately 3m long.

Fossil remains of the freshwater reptile Mesosaurus.

Fossils of the fern Glossopteris, found in all of the southern continents, show that they were once joined.

The discovery of the same fossils in different continents suggested that animals had traveled across the land, which must have all been connected.

CONTINENTAL DRIFT

Continental drift was confirmed when **oceanographers** found ridges on the seafloor in the 1960s, made by magma bubbling up and pushing the land apart. This meant that, up to 250 million years ago, all the continents were joined together as a giant continent called Pangaea. Pangaea split into Gondwanaland and Laurasia and then, 135 million years ago, Gondwanaland split into Africa and South America, while India drifted toward Asia. Finally, 40 million years ago, the continents moved into the positions they are in today.

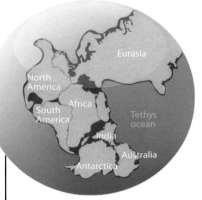

Eurasia

North America

Africa

South America

Tethys ocean

India

Australia

Antarctica

Arctic

North America

Eurasia

Atlantic ocean

South America

Africa

India

Indian ocean

Antarctica

40 MILLION YEARS AGO, AUSTRALIA AND ANTARCTICA SEPARATED WHILE NORTH AMERICA SPLIT FROM EUROPE, LEAVING GREENLAND BEHIND.

It has taken hundreds of millions of years for one continent to split into many.

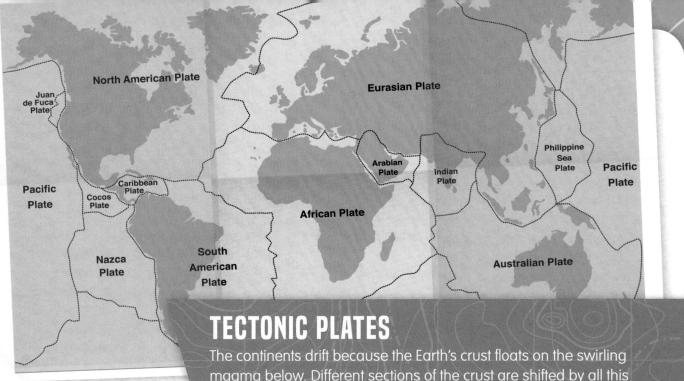

You can see that the continents tend to sit in the middle of the tectonic plates.

TECTONIC PLATES

The continents drift because the Earth's crust floats on the swirling magma below. Different sections of the crust are shifted by all this magma moving around. These sections are called tectonic plates and only move about 2.7 inches (7 cm) a year, the same rate that fingernails grow. They collide, grind sideways, pull apart, or slip under each other. Because they are so massive, the huge amount of pressure causes cracks called faults or fault lines on the Earth's surface.

THE PACIFIC PLATE

The Pacific plate is the largest tectonic plate and sits under the Pacific Ocean. The top part of the plate forms a horseshoe shape called the Ring of Fire. The Ring of Fire has 452 volcanoes dotted along its edge and 90% of the world's earthquakes occur along it. Parts of it are deeper than others, where one plate is sliding underneath another. These long, deep valleys underwater are called trenches.

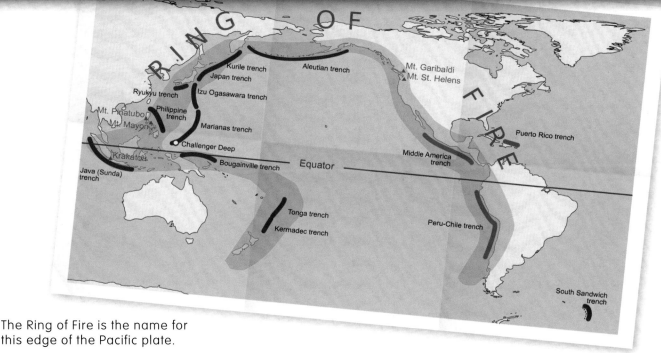

The Ring of Fire is the name for this edge of the Pacific plate.

EARTHQUAKES

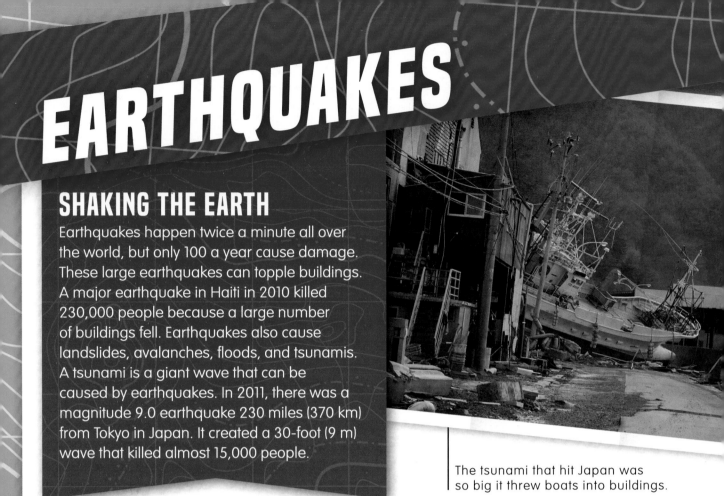

SHAKING THE EARTH

Earthquakes happen twice a minute all over the world, but only 100 a year cause damage. These large earthquakes can topple buildings. A major earthquake in Haiti in 2010 killed 230,000 people because a large number of buildings fell. Earthquakes also cause landslides, avalanches, floods, and tsunamis. A tsunami is a giant wave that can be caused by earthquakes. In 2011, there was a magnitude 9.0 earthquake 230 miles (370 km) from Tokyo in Japan. It created a 30-foot (9 m) wave that killed almost 15,000 people.

The tsunami that hit Japan was so big it threw boats into buildings.

Making Shocks

Most earthquakes happen at a fault line because of tectonic plate movement. The origin of an earthquake, where the rock splits underground, is called the focus. The epicenter is the point on land where a crack appears. Waves of energy called shock waves blast up from the focus to the epicenter, and then travel thousands of miles. Small tremors happen before and after an earthquake and are called foreshocks and aftershocks.

THE SHOCK WAVES OF ENERGY CAN'T BE SEEN, BUT THE TSUNAMI WAVE CAUSED BY THE EARTHQUAKE CAN BE.

The force from the land shifts the water up, creating a giant wave.

MAPPING EARTHQUAKES

Scientists can use maps to track likely earthquakes, using information from fault lines and other **data** to predict where earthquakes are likely to happen. If you know you live somewhere earthquakes are likely, you can build houses and other buildings in such a way that they can withstand an earthquake, and thus be more prepared.

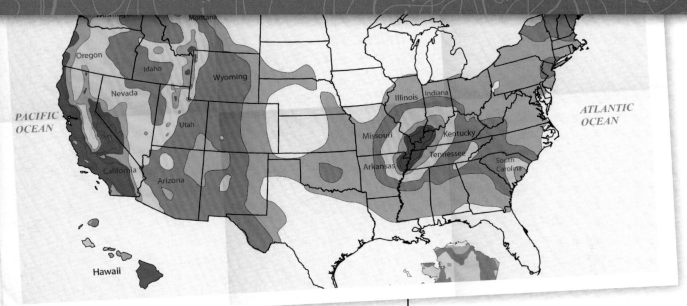

This map shows areas of the U.S. that are most prone to earthquakes. The colors show how many earthquakes, big or small, that area will experience in a year.

Measuring Earthquakes

The Moment Magnitude Scale is used to rate the strength of earthquakes between 1 and 10, with 7 and above being considered major. The Mercalli Scale is used alongside this to describe the damage caused by each category. For example, a magnitude 4.0 earthquake rocks parked cars from side to side. John Milne invented the first device for measuring earthquakes in the 1880s. The seismograph, and modern-day seismometer, move when there are vibrations in the ground. These measurements tell us about seismic activity, which is the movement of rock underground.

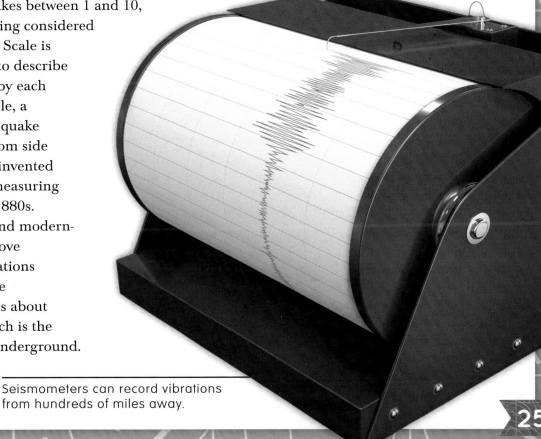

Seismometers can record vibrations from hundreds of miles away.

Making a Mountain

If two tectonic plates collide and the land is folded over and pushed up, it creates fold mountains, such as the Himalayas in Asia. Two plates that force up a huge block of land create block mountains, such as the East African Mountains, or the Sierra Nevada in California. Dome mountains are made by slow-flowing lava, which creates rounded humps, such as the Lake District in England.

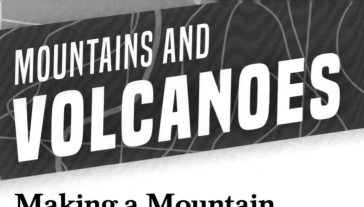

These climbers have set up camp for the night while climbing Mt. Manaslu in the Himalayas.

The Perito Moreno Glacier in Argentina is 18.6 miles (30 km) long. Some glaciers are retreating because they are melting, whereas this one is moving forward.

VALLEYS

Valleys can be made when glaciers move down mountains. A glacier is formed by a lot of snow collecting on the side of a mountain slope. The snow at the bottom is compressed by the weight of the snow above it, which turns it into ice. The heavy block begins to slide down the slope and, as it moves faster, it drags rock with it. The weight of the glacier and the rock grinds out a valley, chewing through the soil like giant teeth.

VOLCANOES

A volcano forms when magma spews out of the ground. The magma is then called lava, which flows and cools, building a cone shape. The flow of lava depends on the rock, gas, and minerals that it is made of. There are thousands of volcanoes, but only 50 to 70 erupt each year.

This is Tungurahua, a volcano in Ecuador.

Mount Vesuvius erupted in AD 79, burying the nearby town of Pompeii, and has erupted several times since. This map shows the lava streams from each eruption in different colors.

MODERN MAPPING SYSTEMS

GIS

Geographical Information Systems (GIS) are maps that have information about an area. It is possible to see different types of information and places using GIS. The data that is included can be anything that happens in that area, so it might be rainfall level, the species of animals found there, or where people live. By showing different types of information, we can see if these things are connected.

By collecting lots of different types of information together onto a map, we can easily see everything in one place.

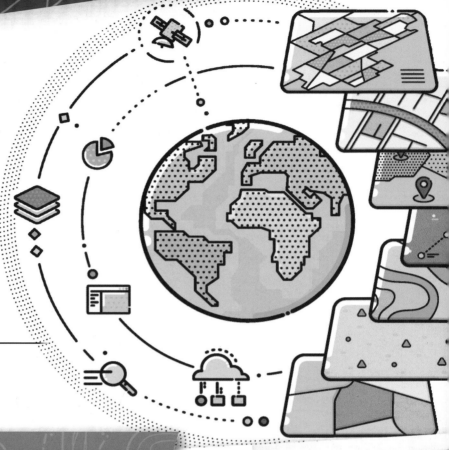

GPS

GPS (Global Positioning System) is a way to locate where someone or something is on the surface of the Earth, using signals from satellites. The first GPS satellite was launched in 1978, and a full network of 24 satellites was completed in 1994. Each satellite lasts 10 years, so new ones have to be launched regularly.

This is a satellite picture of the Ob River, the 7th-longest river in the world, that flows through Russia.

AIRCRAFT AND DRONES, WHICH ARE TYPES OF UNMANNED FLYING VEHICLES, TAKE PICTURES OF THE GROUND AND PIECE THEM TOGETHER.

Maps of the Stars

Sailors and navigators used to use maps of the night sky to work out where they were. By knowing what the night sky should look like in a certain place in the world, they could find their location. Maps of the moon were made in the 1960s to see if a spaceship could land there, in preparation for the first moon landing in 1969.

This is a map of the northern and southern skies at night. By using the calendar, navigators could work out where they were depending on the time of year.

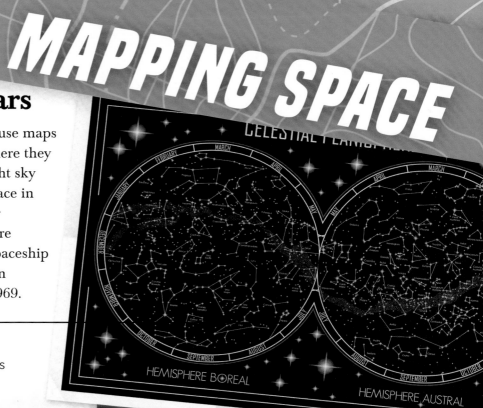

HEMISPHERE BOREAL

HEMISPHERE AUSTRAL

KEEP ON MAPPING

Because of the huge distances involved, we only know a tiny part of the universe and are still trying to map it. The Hubble Space Telescope was launched in 1990 and is still orbiting the Earth, sending back images of deep space. These images are being used to map the universe and understand how planets and suns are made.

A LIGHT-YEAR IS THE DISTANCE LIGHT TRAVELS IN A YEAR. AS LIGHT IS THE FASTEST THING WE KNOW, THIS MEANS ORION NEBULAE IS VERY, VERY FAR AWAY!

This is the Orion Nebulae, which is 1,500 light-years away from Earth.

MAPPING FOR
TREASURE

1. <u>Choose an area to map</u>: Choose somewhere that is small enough so you can add lots of detail and put in a few different features, like your classroom or school playground.

2. <u>Use symbols</u>: You could draw a square for a table or write "Dr" where there is a door.

3. <u>Draw a grid over your map</u>: Make sure the lines are equally spaced.

4. <u>Make a reference</u>: Give each horizontal line a letter, starting with A, and each vertical line a number, starting with 1.

5. <u>Hide the treasure</u>: This could be anything you like! Make a note of the grid reference (see page 14).

6. <u>Ask someone to find the treasure</u>: Give your friend the grid reference of where the treasure is hidden and see if they can find it using your map.

F1

WHEN DRAWING YOUR MAP, TRY TO DRAW IT FROM A BIRD'S-EYE VIEW, AS IF YOU WERE DIRECTLY ABOVE IT LIKE A BIRD AND WERE LOOKING STRAIGHT DOWN.

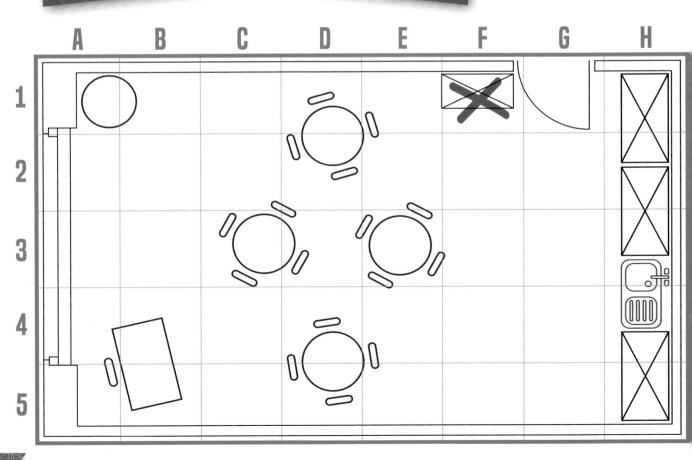

GLOSSARY

three-dimensional (3-D)   something that has depth as well as height and width

architects   people who design buildings

Babylon   an ancient city of southwestern Asia, on the Euphrates River

changeable   likely to change

compresses   presses together

conservationists   people who protect parts of the environment

continents   the seven biggest areas of land in the world

data   information, often numbers

evidence   factual information that proves something

features   defining characteristics

glaciers   a large mass of ice that moves very slowly

hemisphere   one half of the Earth

impassable   impossible to go past

landmarks   features of the landscape used to determine location

livestock   animals that are kept on a farm

navigation   the practice of finding a route, especially when charting a course for a ship or aircraft

oceanographers   people who study the oceans

orbits   moves around a bigger object in space

projection   an image that has been transferred onto a different surface

ratio   a comparison between two things

sea level   the level of the sea's surface

INDEX